Running for Office

John Hamilton

ABDO
Publishing Company

visit us at
www.abdopub.com

Published by ABDO Publishing Company, 4940 Viking Drive, Edina, Minnesota 55435.
Copyright © 2005 by Abdo Consulting Group, Inc. International copyrights reserved in all
countries. No part of this book may be reproduced in any form without written permission from
the publisher. The Checkerboard Library™ is a trademark and logo of ABDO Publishing
Company.

Printed in the United States.

Cover Photos: Corbis
Interior Photos: AP/Wide World pp. 8, 9; Corbis pp. 1, 10, 11, 13, 14, 15, 17, 19, 20, 21, 23, 25,
    26, 27, 29, 31; Getty Images pp. 16, 22; Photo Edit pp. 5, 6, 7, 12, 20

Series Coordinator: Kristin Van Cleaf
Editors: Stephanie Hedlund, Kristin Van Cleaf
Art Direction & Maps: Neil Klinepier

Library of Congress Cataloging-in-Publication Data

Hamilton, John, 1959-
    Running for office / John Hamilton.
        p. cm. -- (Government in action!)
    Includes bibliographical references and index.
    ISBN 1-59197-822-X
    1. Political campaigns--United States--Juvenile literature. 2. Politics, Practical--United
States--Juvenile literature. I. Title. II. Government in action! (ABDO Publishing Company)

JK1978.H34 2005
324.7'0973--dc22

                                                                        2004046289

Contents

Running for Office

During an election year in the United States, television and radio advertisements tell citizens whom to vote for. Signs hang everywhere saying, "Vote for Smith!" or "Jones for City Council!"

These people are running for office. They can do this because they live in a democracy. In this form of government, the people choose other citizens to represent them.

Government positions are filled by public officers such as city council members, mayors, senators, or even the president. These are the people that make and enforce the laws of towns, states, and country. Citizens choose public officers in elections.

To be chosen in an election, a person first needs to be known to the public. He or she does this by running a campaign. Running for public office can be challenging. There are many skills to master. But in the end, the people elected can make a difference in their community and their country.

Opposite page: Many schools hold elections for class officers. So, children can practice running for office, too!

Vote For Katya
Vote FOR kenneth
Vote For Jaqueline M.
VOTE
Vote

Public Office

Assistant Public Administrator

Sheriff-Coroner

MICHAEL S. CARONA
Sheriff

OFFICIAL BALLOT

REPUBLICAN PARTY
Orange C

Many public officers are elected using ballots similar to this one.

The highest law in the United States is the **Constitution**. It is the plan for the country's federal government. But, within the federal government there are many state, city, and town governments. All of them are run by public officers.

These officers keep the government functioning. They make, change, or enforce laws that affect citizens. The people elect most public officers. But, some are appointed to their positions instead.

There are public offices at every level of government. They include state posts, such as governor. Other jobs can be found in county or city governments. Judges and sheriffs are also public officers. Even school districts have elected officials.

The president of the United States is the top public official. Other top jobs include posts in the U.S. Senate and House of Representatives. In all, more than 500,000 Americans are chosen for their jobs through elections.

Judge and sheriff are common local public positions.

Who Can Run?

The people who fill public office positions are ordinary citizens. But to be eligible for these jobs, candidates must first meet certain requirements. Every city and state has different requirements as to who can run for local or state positions.

For example, in the city of Philadelphia, Pennsylvania, the mayor represents approximately 1.5 million people. To qualify for this job, a candidate must be at least 25 years old. He or she must also have lived in the city for at least three years.

To run for governor in Pennsylvania, a person must be at least 30 years old. A candidate must also be a citizen of the United States. And, he or she must have lived in the state of Pennsylvania for at least seven years.

Pennsylvania governor Edward Rendell had to meet his state's requirements before he could run for office.

Public officials often work together. Philadelphia mayor John Street (right) talks with Governor Rendell following Street's swearing-in ceremony.

There are requirements to run for national office, too. To become a U.S. senator, a candidate must be at least 30 years old. He or she must have been a U.S. citizen for at least nine years. A candidate must also be a resident of the state he or she will represent.

To become a U.S. representative, a candidate must be at least 25 years old. He or she must have been a citizen for at least seven years. Like a senator, this person also needs to be a resident of the state he or she will represent.

Eliot Spitzer's degree from Harvard Law School qualified him to become attorney general of New York.

To run for president of the United States, a man or woman must be at least 35 years old. He or she must have been a resident of the United States for at least 14 years. The candidate must also be a natural-born citizen. However, there is disagreement as to what this means. Some people are unsure whether this includes a person born in a foreign country to parents who are U.S. citizens.

Special training is usually not required to run for public office. Usually, a person must simply meet age and residency requirements. Some offices that do require special training include **attorneys general** and **district attorneys**. To qualify for these jobs, a candidate must be a lawyer.

John F. Kennedy gives a speech at his inauguration in 1961. At age 43, Kennedy was the youngest person to be elected president of the United States.

Political Parties

People who run for public office usually belong to political parties. Political parties are groups of people interested in politics and society. They are like clubs where everyone has similar ideas on how the government should be run.

The logo of the Green Party, a popular third party

In the United States, the two most important political parties are the Republican Party and the Democratic Party. The Republican Party supports conservative social policies. Republicans believe in limited federal government. They also believe state and local problems should be fixed locally.

On the other hand, Democrats are more liberal. They believe it's the federal government's main job to help solve problems. Democrats think issues are best solved by passing federal laws that state and local governments must follow.

There are other parties in the United States as well. They are known as third parties. Candidates from these smaller parties do not often win election to higher office. However, they can influence the major parties. Two of the main third parties today are the Reform Party and the Green Party.

Candidates usually have the support of a political party. This provides candidates with some **credibility**. Most often, a Republican or a Democrat will win a position in Congress or the presidency.

A third-party candidate has not yet become president. However third-party members, such as former Minnesota governor Jesse Ventura of the Independent Party, have been elected to other important positions.

DEMOCRATIC PARTY

- ★ Symbol is the donkey
- ★ Favors using tax money to pay for government programs
- ★ Believes that the government should make sure businesses are fair
- ★ Focuses on the power of the government to make decisions
- ★ Supports a strong national government
- ★ Supports the rights of workers
- ★ Believes all people should have the same rights and opportunities

REPUBLICAN PARTY

- ★ *Symbol is the elephant*
- ★ *Favors lower taxes, leaving more money in the hands of the people*
- ★ *Believes that businesses are most successful when government is not involved*
- ★ *Focuses on the power of individuals to make decisions*
- ★ *Supports strong local governments*
- ★ *Supports free trade*
- ★ *Believes all people should have the same rights and opportunities*

Getting Started

Before the campaign even begins, there is a lot of work to do. In the beginning, candidates study a lot of information. They look at **opinion polls** and an area's **economic** and social conditions. Such information helps them determine the issues that their community is dealing with.

From this research, candidates can decide what their positions are on these issues. Candidates may sometimes base their positions on their party's platform. A platform is a statement of the party's views and goals on important national issues.

Arianna Huffington announces her decision to run for governor of California.

A woman signs a petition in support of Ross Perot's candidacy.

To mark their official start, candidates announce that they are running for office. This is called declaring their candidacy. Candidates often do this at a **media** event.

In some states, candidates must also petition to be put on the **ballot**. A petition is a collection of **signatures**. It shows that the candidate has the support of local voters. Some positions require a certain amount of signatures before a person can run. Such laws are different in every state.

The Campaign

Once a candidate has enough **signatures**, he or she files for office. This involves filling out the proper forms. Many public offices also require candidates to pay a filing fee. Then, the actual campaigning begins.

A campaign is an organized plan for seeking office. Candidates campaign in order to tell people about themselves and their ideas. They hope to convince enough supporters to vote them into office.

To get the campaign going, candidates start raising money. Running a political campaign can be expensive. Money is needed to pay for staff, advertising, and other events. Presidential candidates spend hundreds of millions of dollars during presidential elections.

Most of the money used in campaigns comes from voluntary contributions. Individuals, political parties, or large groups can donate this money. Presidential candidates can also receive public funds. Citizens donate this money when they file their taxes.

Candidates will often hold fancy dinners to raise funds for their campaigns. Here, George W. Bush speaks at a fund-raiser for his 2004 campaign.

Candidates can also use an unlimited amount of their own money. However, laws control how much money a candidate can receive from other sources. The laws also regulate where money can come from and how it can be spent. These laws try to keep campaigns fair.

At the same time candidates are raising money, they are also hiring a campaign staff. This includes a campaign manager and a staff of paid positions. Volunteers are also needed. These people carry out the everyday workings of a campaign.

The campaign manager works on a **strategy**. He or she will develop the campaign's message. This is a brief summary of the candidate's goals and reasons why voters should support him or her. The manager also tries to create a theme for people to follow throughout the campaign.

A poster advertises John F. Kennedy's campaign in 1960.

The staff helps arrange rallies, **debates**, and public visits. Volunteers help candidates by going door-to-door, or by phoning people and asking for their vote. They may hang up posters or hand out flyers and other campaign literature. Other supporters may set out lawn signs to advertise their candidate.

Staff members do research for Howard Dean's campaign in 2004.

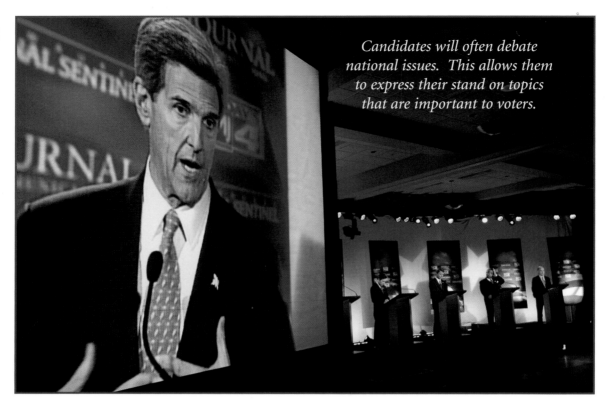

Candidates will often debate national issues. This allows them to express their stand on topics that are important to voters.

Campaigns also make use of the **media**. This is where most public opinion is formed today. Candidates place advertisements on television and radio. Advertisements are also seen in newspapers, books, and magazines. Internet Web sites are important in reaching voters, too.

Another use of media includes sound bites. These are short, easily remembered statements containing the important points of a candidate's campaign. Candidates use sound bites in their speeches and public statements. They hope the media will use these statements in their reports on a campaign's progress.

Campaigners look for supporters as they pass along their candidate's message. They send information to voters and ask for their active support. This could mean donating money, volunteering, or just voting.

In 1960, Richard M. Nixon (left) and John F. Kennedy participated in the first televised debates. Here, Nixon debates from Los Angeles while Kennedy debates from New York.

Choosing One

Any number of candidates can run for the same public office. In presidential campaigns, one party may have as many as a dozen candidates. To choose the party's official nominee for an office, political parties hold caucuses and primary elections.

A caucus is a private meeting of local party members. The members **debate** and then choose their nominee. However, primaries are more common today. A primary is a special election within a political party. Voters choose the candidate they want to represent their party in the general election.

Presidential elections are held every four years in November. So, primaries are usually held in the previous winter through late spring. But, each state decides when and how its primaries will be held.

After the primaries, the national parties hold national **conventions**. These are usually in July and August. At the conventions, each party chooses one official candidate to represent the party in the general election.

Party members celebrate Bill Clinton's nomination for presidential candidate at the 1996 Democratic National Convention.

Conventions are made up of each state's official delegates, as well as the **media** and **lobbyists**. Delegates traditionally vote for the candidate who won their home state's primary election. Most often, the candidate who won the most state primary elections will win the national nomination.

Election Day

Candidate Howard Dean hands out cups of coffee to voters, campaign staff, and poll workers at a polling place in New Hampshire.

Campaigning goes on for many months, both before and after the **conventions**. All of this campaigning prepares the candidate for Election Day. For most positions, Election Day is on the first Tuesday after the first Monday in November.

On this day, citizens vote for their favorite candidate. People vote at official locations called **polling places**. These are usually public places such as schools, fire stations, or churches.

Candidates continue their campaigns on Election Day in hopes of gaining last-minute votes. They may visit polling places and talk with voters. Campaign staff may stand outside the polls and hand out information to voters.

Many states have laws about campaigning on Election Day. Political candidates may only campaign if they do not prevent voters from entering or exiting the **polling place**. In some areas, political signs or banners are not allowed within a certain distance of the polls.

That night, candidates host parties for their families, friends, and campaign supporters. While they wait to hear the results of the election, they thank everyone for their work. After the polling places close, the votes are counted and reported to election officials. Often, the winner is declared that night.

John Kerry celebrates his victory in a primary election.

Getting Involved

People run for office because they have an interest in government. They see something they want to change. Or, they want more of a say in how things are run.

Democracy allows ordinary citizens to be a part of this process. They have the freedom to take part in the government if they wish. They can vote in elections or even become public officers themselves.

Even if a person can't run for office, he or she can still be a part of the democratic process. Many schools and communities have political clubs. Political parties are always looking for members. It is even possible to volunteer to work on a campaign.

Getting involved in the government is one way people can make a difference. And, running for office is just the first step. Once elected, officials are able to serve the people. They are actively supporting their government and the United States.

Opposite page: *Children attend a rally to support Arnold Schwarzenegger's campaign for governor of California.*

Glossary

attorney general - the chief law officer of a national or state government.

ballot - to vote. It is also a piece of paper used to cast a vote.

Constitution - the laws that govern the United States.

convention - a large meeting set up for a special purpose.

credibility - the quality of being believable or reliable.

debate - to discuss a question or topic, often publicly.

district attorney - a lawyer for the government who works in a specific district, such as a county or state.

economy - the way a nation uses its money, goods, and natural resources.

lobby - to influence lawmakers to vote a certain way. A person who does this is called a lobbyist.

media - communications companies, such as the news media.

opinion poll - a survey of people's opinions on a certain topic.

polling place - the site where votes are cast in an election.

signature - a person's name written in his or her own handwriting.

strategy - a plan of action.

Web Sites

To learn more about running for office, visit ABDO Publishing Company on the World Wide Web at **www.abdopub.com**. Web sites about campaigns and elections are featured on our Book Links page. These links are routinely monitored and updated to provide the most current information available.

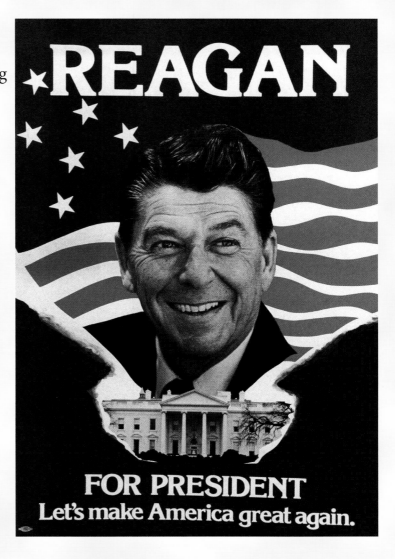

Index